HAMMOND PUBLIC LIBRARY

3 1161 00777 5946

S0-BDL-544

y591.97287 INTO 2004
Into wild Panama

JUL 22 2004

HAMMOND PUBLIC LIBRARY
INDIANA
(219) 931-5100

HPL   HPY   EBH
HOW   CLC

THIS BOOK IS RENEWABLE BY PHONE OR IN
PERSON IF THERE IS NO RESERVE WAITING.
DEMCO

Amhurst, IN

INTO
Wild Panama

**BLACKBIRCH®
PRESS**

San Diego • Detroit • New York • San Francisco • Cleveland • New Haven, Conn. • Waterville, Maine • London • Munich

Hammond Public Library
Hammond, IN

THOMSON

GALE

© 2004 by Blackbirch Press™. Blackbirch Press™ is an imprint of The Gale Group, Inc., a division of Thomson Learning, Inc.

Blackbirch Press™ and Thomson Learning™ are trademarks used herein under license.

For more information, contact
The Gale Group, Inc.
27500 Drake Rd.
Farmington Hills, MI 48331-3535
Or you can visit our Internet site at http://www.gale.com

ALL RIGHTS RESERVED
No part of this work covered by the copyright hereon may be reproduced or used in any form or by any means—graphic, electronic, or mechanical, including photocopying, recording, taping, Web distribution or information storage retrieval systems—without the written permission of the publisher.

Every effort has been made to trace the owners of copyrighted material.

Photo credits: cover, pages all © Discovery Communications, Inc. except for pages 6–7, 12, 25, 45 © Blackbirch Press Archives. Images on bottom banner © PhotoDisc, Corel Corporation, and Powerphoto; page 39 © PhotoDisc; page 40 © photos.com

Discovery Communications, Discovery Communications logo, TLC (The Learning Channel), TLC (The Learning Channel) logo, Animal Planet, and the Animal Planet logo are trademarks of Discovery Communications Inc., used under license.

LIBRARY OF CONGRESS CATALOGING-IN-PUBLICATION DATA

Into wild Panama / Elaine Pascoe, book editor.
    p. cm. — (The Jeff Corwin experience)
Based on an episode from a Discovery Channel program hosted by Jeff Corwin.
Summary: Television personality Jeff Corwin takes the reader on an expedition to Panama to learn about the diverse wildlife found there.
Includes bibliographical references and index.
    ISBN 1-56711-856-9 (hardback : alk. paper) — ISBN 1-4103-0176-1 (pbk. : alk. paper)
1. Zoology—Panama—Juvenile literature. [1. Zoology—Panama. 2. Panama—Description and travel. 3. Corwin, Jeff.] I. Pascoe, Elaine. II. Corwin, Jeff. III. Series.

QL228.P2I58 2004
591.97287—dc21   2003009274

Printed in China
10 9 8 7 6 5 4 3 2 1

Y591.97287
JNTO
2004

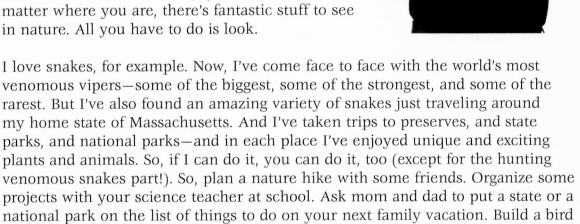

E ver since I was a kid, I dreamed about traveling around the world, visiting exotic places, and seeing all kinds of incredible animals. And now, guess what? That's exactly what I get to do!

Yes, I am incredibly lucky. But, you don't have to have your own television show on Animal Planet to go off and explore the natural world around you. I mean, I travel to Madagascar and the Amazon and all kinds of really cool places—but I don't need to go that far to see amazing wildlife up close. In fact, I can find thousands of incredible critters right here, in my own backyard—or in my neighbor's yard (he does get kind of upset when he finds me crawling around in the bushes, though). The point is, no matter where you are, there's fantastic stuff to see in nature. All you have to do is look.

I love snakes, for example. Now, I've come face to face with the world's most venomous vipers—some of the biggest, some of the strongest, and some of the rarest. But I've also found an amazing variety of snakes just traveling around my home state of Massachusetts. And I've taken trips to preserves, and state parks, and national parks—and in each place I've enjoyed unique and exciting plants and animals. So, if I can do it, you can do it, too (except for the hunting venomous snakes part!). So, plan a nature hike with some friends. Organize some projects with your science teacher at school. Ask mom and dad to put a state or a national park on the list of things to do on your next family vacation. Build a bird house. Whatever. But get out there.

As you read through these pages and look at the photos, you'll probably see how jazzed I get when I come face to face with beautiful animals. That's good. I want you to feel that excitement. And I want you to remember that—even if you don't have your own TV show—you can still experience the awesome beauty of nature almost anywhere you go—any day of the week. I only hope that I can help bring that awesome power and beauty a little closer to you. Enjoy!

Best Wishes!
Jeff

INTO Wild Panama

ASIA

NORTH
AMERICA

EUROPE

Atlantic
Ocean

Pacific
Ocean

AFRICA

Indian
Ocean

SOUTH
AMERICA

Pacific
Ocean

AUSTRALIA

This is where north meets south, where two continents collide. We're on a bridge between the Americas, in a tropical paradise filled with creatures of all shapes and sizes.

I'm Jeff Corwin.
Welcome to Panama.

Join me as we explore the narrow strip of land in Central America known as Panama. When people think of this country, what immediately comes to mind is the Panama Canal, one of the greatest man-made wonders of the world. But Panama's natural wonders are not to be overshadowed.

Looking at the canal...

That's all dry stuff there.

Look up! It's a rufous-naped tamarind!

We're beginning our Panama visit not far from the famous canal, in this beautiful forest. It's extraordinarily dry here, and the leaf litter underfoot is all crunchy. This forest is usually moist, but this is what it's like in the dry season.

Speaking of things crunching through the leaf litter, I just caught sight of the tail of a very fat snake. And I'm not the only creature that saw it. A band of rufous-naped tamarinds

Corwin to the rescue...

He's a beautiful boa.

spotted the snake, too, and now they're squawking and squeaking because this creature frequently preys on tamarinds. I think they're saying, "Please, get that snake! Get it out of here!" I'm on it. I hope they know there's a fee involved... two bananas.

I have him, and he's a beautiful snake, a boa constrictor imperator. You can find this species of snake living from Mexico all the way down to Argentina. What's interesting is that each region has its own unique phase, or coloration, almost like a subspecies. This individual has a really neat pattern I've never seen before. It's a light tan, not the rich, dark brown you see in South American boas. It's lighter, with iridescent saddles.

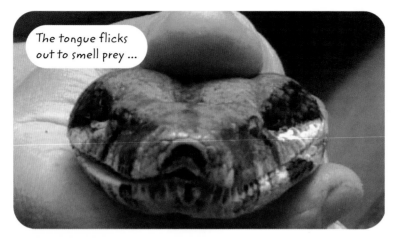

The tongue flicks out to smell prey ...

... and then ... Wham!

Like other boas and pythons, this snake kills its prey not with venom, as a rattlesnake would do, but with constriction—with a deadly squeeze. When it's hunting, it first detects the prey with its tongue. The tongue flicks in and out of its mouth, picking up the chemical trails of potential prey such as young agouti or a rufous-naped tamarind. The boa tracks down its prey and then waits, perfectly still, allowing its coloration to blend in with its surroundings so that it almost disappears. And then—wham! The snake reaches out, grabs on, coils around the prey, and squeezes until it's dead. Then it swallows the prey whole.

This body is full of powerful coils.

This is the largest snake in Central America.

These boa constrictors are the largest snakes in Central America, and they're beautiful serpents. I'm noticing some interesting things about this individual. Look where my finger's pointing, and you'll see something that almost looks like a raised scale. It's not a scale; it's an ectoparasite, a tick, that's going along for a free ride and a meal of the snake's blood.

Normally, if we were just observing this snake, I probably would not move him. But because I exposed snake to tamarind, tamarind to snake, I don't want to be a part of this creature consuming those animals. So I'm going to move him away, just a little bit, and let him go.

It's amazing to think that I'm just five miles outside this nation's bustling capital, Panama City. This is a relatively new forest, just eighty years old, and it is the only link between the city and the Panama Canal watershed. Despite its youth, this forest is filled with wild creatures.

This forest is home to tons of creatures.

Look at this! This extraordinary creature is a sloth, and here's what's really cool about it: 99 percent of its life is spent upside down, hanging from tree branches. It eats, it sleeps, and—if it's a female—it gives birth upside down.

Sloths are so cool ...

Which one of us is upside down?

Can you guess if this is a two-toed or a three-toed sloth?

There are two different species of sloths that make their home in Panama, the three-toed and the two-toed. Just look at the front limb of this guy and you will see two digitlike talons, which tells you he's a two-toed sloth. Sloths are herbivores, eating leaves. The three-toed sloth is very specific about what it likes to eat, and the leaves it prefers are those of the cecropia tree. But this guy is more of a generalist—there are more plants that are part of his diet.

Often, living in the fur of these two-toed sloths is a type of algae, which gives the fur a greenish cast. This algae is found nowhere else

but on two-toed sloth fur. And here's something else that's neat about these animals. Not only do they harbor this unique species of algae in their fur, but they also harbor a

A special algae grows on this fur.

moth that lives in the fur and eats the algae. So you have an animal living in this complex ecosystem, and in itself it's a complex microecosystem, home to all sorts of flora and fauna. Sloths— wonderful creatures, very bizarre and very adorable. This is what I love about Panama.

Bizarre, yet adorable.

The Panama Canal is a busy place.

Bridge of the Americas.

Everybody who passes through this system of locks, making their way along the Panama Canal, has to pay a fee. The canal is a very expensive operation, so passage isn't free. But the prices vary. Little boats may pay only a couple of hundred dollars. But giant cargo ships sometimes pay as much as $180,000 dollars.

We're near the Pacific end of the Panama Canal, which stretches more than 50 miles plus to the Atlantic. Here the Bridge of the Americas unites both banks of the canal. The bridge was built for the passage of human beings. But prior to the building of the Panama Canal, there was a land bridge here. And animals had been crossing that natural bridge for millions of years, going from south to north and north to south.

Before the creation of the Panama Canal, this region consisted mostly of rain forest. But in 1913 it was flooded, creating Gatun Lake. The lake is dotted with islands that were once mountaintops. And ever since the lake was created, the animals on these mountaintop islands have been isolated. It's a great place to explore and find interesting creatures.

Our first stop is Tigre Island, actually a small chain of islands in Gatun Lake. It's a primate sanctuary, and it gives us a great opportunity to see some really cool New

Let's go play with some primates!

World monkeys up close. The only problem is, monkeys always seem to give me trouble. We'll see what happens.

Look at this—the monkeys have sent the welcome wagon. Hello, ladies and gentlemen. We have two different species of monkeys here. The black ones are Colombian black-headed monkeys, which are spider monkeys from South America, and the others are Central American spider monkeys. It's only in Panama that you see the two species together— the Colombian species moving northward, and the Central American species moving southward. That's an example of what has been occurring in this land for

These guys are the Central American monkeys.

This is a Colombian spider monkey.

millions of years—the exchange of species, through the great funnel of Panama.

This one doesn't like me too much ...

I'm keeping my eye on this Colombian monkey because he's not happy we're on this island. He's tough—he's showing his teeth, smacking the branches around, and trying to make himself larger than life. But look at the way he swings through the trees—look how agile he is. And he's doing that with four fingers, not the thumb. Why? Because he doesn't have a thumb. He doesn't need one. Thumbs would just get in the way as he jumps and swings through the trees.

Look, no thumb!

Night monkeys are so cute—don't you think?

In front of me are two night monkeys, absolutely adorable primates. They're probably the second smallest species of primate living in Central America, and easily one of the smallest in the New World tropics. They usually move in small groups, in family units of two to four individuals, sleeping in tree hollows during the daytime hours. Then they wake up, punch in for the night shift, and go to work. They run around, hopping from branch to branch and from tree to tree, foraging for sap, fruits, and tender shoots. They eat insects and, sometimes, even small animals. And they are just adorable.

A very small island nearby is home to a colony of rufous-naped tamarinds, those little monkeys that we saw earlier on the mainland. They're the smallest primates in Central America.

Twin baby tamarinds!

And look at this—twins! Aren't these babies adorable? They hold on to their mother's back, but when they feel secure they get off and nibble on some bananas.

These little primates are named for that reddish mane on the back of their neck. Their diet is 60 percent fruit, 30 percent insects, and 10 percent nectar. They can live for fifteen years plus, and they live very well in the presence of human beings—as long as human beings aren't exploiting them for food or the pet industry.

These tamarinds are perfect subjects for research scientists.

Since these tamarinds have been living in the isolated environment of this island, they're excellent candidates for research study. That's why they're wearing identification collars, which also happen to double as very chic necklaces.

Snazzy jewelry, don't you think?

From the top of the forest canopy, we're getting a view into a tropical rain forest that most people never have a chance to experience. I was hoisted up here by a canopy crane. This particular crane was built through a cooperative effort between the Smithsonian Institution and UNEP, the United Nations Environmental Program. And it affords scientists a rare opportunity to study a rain forest completely, from top to bottom. The crane is 140 feet tall, but it also can extend out 140 feet.

This is an awesome view.

Goin' up ...

Iguanas like this live in the canopy.

I can see Panama City!

The canopy is the part of the forest where 80 percent of the tropical life forms live. It's where the primates live, where the sloths live, and where many of the lizards and frogs live. In fact, right there is a green iguana, having an afternoon snack on some tender leaves.

From up here, it is a shock to see how close the city is. The rain forest smacks right into Panama's urban jungle. It's a meeting of two totally different worlds, with sometimes unpleasant consequences.

Just a few miles out of Panama's capital and it's a rain-forest wilderness.

José Luis and I look at this baby coati.

Isn't this creature the sweetest?

Ancon is a nonprofit organization that specializes in conserving the natural resources of Panama. It also reaches out to the community to educate people. And it reaches out to the community in another way, through José Luis Ortega.

José Luis works with an Ancon program called the Green Line. He rescues wildlife like this beautiful little coati—wildlife that finds its way into the habitat of human beings. This little animal, a relative of the raccoon, was orphaned when its mother was shot.

Panama City is surrounded by beautiful tropical rain-forest habitat. And because of that, there is always contact between wildlife and human beings. Often the ending of the encounter is tragic—the animal is killed, or sometimes people can be injured. But that's where José Luis comes in. His job is basically to rescue animals and prevent a tragic ending.

One of the animals in José Luis's care is a tamandua, a type of anteater, that somehow found his way into a kitchen. We'll release this tamandua far enough away so it won't find its way back into any more kitchen sinks. These guys are fast, and they climb very quickly. But we'll get a good look at him before he goes.

Ever seen a tamandua?

Looks like an anteater ... because it is.

These guys are related to sloths and armadillos.

Look at that nose, the anteater nose. Anteaters belong to a group of mammals called xenarthrans, a group that includes sloths and armadillos. These creatures have been moving for millions of years across the great land bridge called the Isthmus of Panama, but most of the types live in South America and in Central America. The only xenarthran ever to make it to North America, at least in modern days, is the armadillo.

These claws are like razors.

This animal's feet end in extremely sharp claws. When he wants to defend himself, he rears up and holds out his arms—he can't bite but he can slash

with those claws. These guys spend a lot of time in trees, and they have prehensile tails that they use like a fifth limb, to grab onto the branches. They use their claws to climb and, most importantly, to rip apart the homes of the creatures they eat.

When it's time for this animal to feed, he approaches a termite nest or an anthill and starts to dig. Then he sticks his muzzle in and flicks out his sticky tongue to pick up ants. He may get to eat for only a few minutes, because then the soldiers come out— the large ants that spe-

This creature loves to eat insects.

cialize in defense and can deliver bites and stings. The tamandua will either close his eyes and tolerate the stings for a little bit, or move off and then possibly return to the nest later. He's an extraordinary creature, primitive in design, but perfect for survival in this tough ecosystem.

Ocelots are gorgeous.

These cats are great climbers.

Here is a native predator that is somewhat tolerant of humans, and I'd really like you to see him. It's a beautiful cat, an ocelot. These creatures are as comfortable up in the trees as they are moving along the ground. Look at his beautiful coloration. Those spots break up his shape, allowing him to blend in with his surroundings. I have to keep a sharp eye on this tom because one minute he's happy, exploring, and playing around—and the next minute, he could be using my leg as a scratching post.

Ocelots are the largest of the small-bodied cats in the New World tropics. The small-bodied cats include creatures like margays, jaguarundis (not jaguars), little tiger cats, and ocelots. A male ocelot like this can weigh up to 35 pounds, which makes his species the largest of the group.

Despite his size, this guy is an amazing, stealthy carnivore. He'll take all sorts of prey and go just about anywhere to get it. He'll go in the river after turtles and fish and frogs. He'll climb up a tree to go after tree rats or birds.

Ocelots like to eat meat—and they can go anywhere to get it.

Ocelots have been spotted from Arizona through Mexico, and all the way down through Central and South America. They originated in North America and they spread south by crossing the Isthmus of Panama. The land bridge rose out of the ocean a couple of million years ago, and ocelots have basically been making their way from North America to South America ever since—while creatures like armadillos and anteaters were moving north.

Let's see here ...

Can you see the snake?

Besides the surly ocelot, this area has another wild resident I want you to see. This is one of the most wonderful serpents living in the neotropics, a gorgeous snake. You can usually find it close to the roots of a tree, where it blends in perfectly with fallen leaves.

This snake shares ancestry with the North American

Here he is ...

... and look at that spear-shaped head.

rattlesnake. It's a *Bothrops asper*, or fer-de-lance, an absolutely beautiful serpent. The name fer-de-lance refers to the shape of this creature's head, which looks like the tip of a spear or a lance.

I'm holding him carefully because he's armed with fangs, and he's venomous. As with all the vipers, he has solenoglyphous fangs, and that's pretty neat. It means that the fangs are hinged, and the snake can extend them, rotate them, and retract them. When this creature reaches out to grasp its prey, it stretches its mouth open wide, digs those fangs in, and then pulls forward. As it does that, it

This snake's fangs can move in and out.

See the hole? It's a heat sensor.

pumps out copious amounts of venom, which starts to destroy the tissue of its prey to make digestion easier for the serpent.

Here's something else that is amazing about this snake, a characteristic it shares with the rattlesnakes and the copperheads. Behind its nares, or nostrils, is a hole. It's a thermal receptor site. It gives this creature the amazing ability to detect the warmth that radiates from warm-blooded prey, such as rodents and birds. Once it detects prey, it can sit perfectly still, waiting to strike. The camouflage it uses to hide from predators is also the camouflage it uses to hunt, so it is not detected by its prey.

The beautiful fer-de-lance is venomous and potentially dangerous—but, treated with respect, it earns a lot of admiration. It certainly has an important place in this ecosystem.

Heading to the Darién.

Just a short flight from Panama City is an area called the Darién. A hundred years ago, humans tried to settle this area—but the jungle resisted and eventually won. Today the only human residents are some biologists.

This is a very wild jungle.

Going to the cave ...

Chichile, one of the workers at the Ancon Field Station here, is taking us to an old mine shaft that is home to some mysterious frogs. I've been told they're big and purple, and they've only been seen in this cave. I'm going to try to identify them after we wade through what looks like three feet of bat guano on the floor of the cave.

... slugging through the guano.

Now, look at the size of this frog—he's huge. But he's not so mysterious. He's a smoky frog *(Leptodactylus pentadactylus)*, an animal

found throughout South America. This is the first time I've seen one in Central America, though, and I've never seen one this big. Check out his pectoral muscles; he could pop a cap off a soda bottle. And look at those arms. The spines on his chest tell me that it's mating season—the spines actually help the male hold on when he mounts the female.

Out in the forest, you'd find these guys eating insects. But in this cave system, they're eating bats. Cool frogs. It was great that we could come here and solve this little mystery.

Check out the pecs on this smokey frog.

These guys have a taste for bats.

Some poison dart frogs are brightly colored, to warn predators.

Check out this little frog.

See the bubbling back? Those are tadpoles waiting to hatch.

Here's an amazing creature—one of the smallest species of dendrobates, or poison dart frogs, living in the Americas. I have to be careful with him because he's really fragile. But these animals have an excellent defense. They manufacture a deadly toxin in their skin. If a predator were to eat this frog, or if the toxin entered its bloodstream in another way, it would probably die.

There's something else that's amazing about this frog. This is a male, and he's transporting his tadpoles on his back. Just look at that. Its back is bubbling with a new generation of

This dad is taking his offspring to a nice place...

... like this bromeliad plant.

poison dart frogs. When they hatch, these tadpoles wriggle onto the frog's back and stick to a mucus the frog secretes. He transports them to good locations for growing up, such as the water-holding funnels of bromeliad plants. A wonderful, tiny creature, and something to remember—the poison dart frog.

Yikes!

Eyelash vipers are very, very venomous.

This spectacular snake is an eyelash viper. Although they're not particularly aggressive, these vipers are very, very venomous— and they have a very good reach. They're also excellent climbers. I have to be very careful handling this snake. About a third of all viper bites are dry, meaning venom isn't delivered. But those aren't good odds in my book. That's why you have to be so careful when you're working with venomous snakes. If you screw up, you can be dead. And you can't blame the snake.

Look right above his eyes, where you can see the row of scales. That's why this snake is called the eyelash viper, not because it has

Excellent camouflage ...

... and beautiful scales.

hair. Reptiles don't have hair; they have scales. And look at the camouflage. These are the prettiest vipers you'll find in the New World. They come in all sorts of colors—orange, yellow, green. This one is cinnamon.

The one I caught was cinnamon colored.

No matter how much of an unnatural fear of snakes is coiled up in your body, when you look at this creature you can't help but see a beautiful animal. It's a wonderful venomous snake. And that's what's great about exploring the Darién—there are tons of things to be found here.

Harpy eagles are the largest New World eagles.

Wow! What a raptor.

Look at this magnificent creature. It's a harpy eagle, probably the greatest raptor and certainly the largest eagle in the New World. This bird has the ability to pull a sloth right out of the

These talons are deadly weapons.

canopy with her powerful talons. Look how she grips that glove. The talons of harpy eagles can be five inches long, and they're designed to crunch bone, pierce a spine, rip through flesh, and snatch an animal that weighs 20 pounds or more right out of its tree.

You're probably wondering how I ended up with this harpy eagle on my arm. We certainly didn't track it in the wild. This individual is part of a worldwide conservation program, the Peregrine Fund, operating here in Panama.

These birds are top predators in the rain forest.

Just two buddies ...

The Peregrine Fund specializes in the conservation of raptors.

These eagles are extremely powerful—powerful in flight, powerful in the way they take their prey. Essentially they are the jaguars of the canopy, at the top of the food pyramid up there. The harpy eagle is an amazing creature, and I think it's a wonderful way to wrap up our visit. Not only is it an extraordinary beast, but it is also the national bird of Panama.

Hope you had a great time here in wild Panama. I'll see you on our next adventure!

Glossary

canopy the top layer of a rain forest

carnivore an animal that eats meat

conservation preservation or protection

constriction squeezing or compression

copious a large amount

ecosystem a community of organisms

guano bat droppings

habitat a place where animals and plants live naturally together

herbivore an animal that eats plants

iridescent shiny or sparkling

mammals warm-blooded animals that feed their babies with milk

nectar a sweet liquid produced by some plants

predator an animal that kills and eats other animals

prehensile the ability to grasp or wrap around

primate a type of mammal such as a monkey, an ape, or a human

rain forest a tropical forest that receives a lot of rain

raptor a type of bird that hunts and eats other animals, such as an eagle

sanctuary a place where animals are safe and protected

serpent a snake

talon an animal's claw

venom a poison used by snakes to attack their prey or defend themselves

viper a type of venomous snake

watershed a place that drains into a body of water

Index

3 1161 00777 5946